MARSUPIALS

by
Madeline Tyler

KidHaven
PUBLISHING

Published in 2020 by KidHaven Publishing, an Imprint of Greenhaven Publishing, LLC
353 3rd Avenue, Suite 255, New York, NY 10010

Written by: Madeline Tyler
Edited by: John Wood
Designed by: Danielle Jones

Names: Tyler, Madeline.
Title: Marsupials / Madeline Tyler.
Description: New York : KidHaven Publishing, 2020. | Series: Animal classification | Includes glossary and index.
Identifiers: ISBN 9781534530584 (pbk.) | ISBN 9781534530263 (library bound) | ISBN 9781534531352 (6 pack)
| ISBN 9781534530485 (ebook)
Subjects: LCSH: Marsupials--Juvenile literature.
Classification: LCC QL737.M3 T95 2020 | DDC 599.2--dc23

PHOTO CREDITS

Printed in the United States of America

CPSIA compliance information: Batch #BS19KL: For further information contact Greenhaven Publishing LLC, New York, New York at
1-844-317-7404.

CONTENTS

Words that look like <u>this</u> are explained in the glossary on page 31.

THE ANIMAL KINGDOM

The animal kingdom includes over 8 million known living <u>species</u>. They come in many different shapes and sizes, they each do weird and wonderful things, and they live all over planet Earth.

From the freezing Arctic waters to the hottest desert in the world, animals have <u>adapted</u> to the often extreme and diverse conditions on Earth.

Even though each and every species of animal is <u>unique</u>, they still share certain characteristics with each other. These shared characteristics are used to classify animals. There are six main groups used to classify animals: mammals, reptiles, birds, invertebrates, amphibians, and fish.

10,000 new species of animal are discovered **every year.**

Some smaller animal classification groups include marsupials and mollusks. Marsupials include kangaroos, wallabies, koalas, wombats, and possums.

MARSUPIALS

WHAT IS A MARSUPIAL?

A marsupial is a type of animal. Most marsupials live in Australia, but a few species live in Central and South America.

Only one species, the Virginia opossum, lives in North America. Marsupials are mammals that give birth to <u>young</u> which are very <u>premature</u>. They are all <u>warm-blooded</u> and produce milk for their young. Most marsupials have a pouch. Young marsupials live in the pouch until they are big enough to explore outside.

Female wallabies keep their young, called joeys, safe in their pouches.

There are around 334 species of marsupials in the world. Although marsupials are similar to each other, they have all adapted differently for their habitats. Some marsupials live high up in the trees and others live in burrows under the ground.

Eastern Pygmy Possum

Red Kangaroo

The largest marsupial in the world is the red kangaroo, which can grow up to 5.2 feet (1.6 m) tall. One of the smallest marsupials on Earth is the eastern pygmy possum. Their bodies only grow 2.7 to 4.3 inches (7 to 11 cm) long.

MARSUPIAL CHECKLIST

- 🐾 Give birth to premature young
- 🐾 Produce milk
- 🐾 Covered in fur

- 🐾 <u>Vertebrate</u>
- 🐾 Have a pouch
- 🐾 Warm-blooded
- 🐾 Breathe air using lungs

BODY PARTS

Marsupials come in all sorts of shapes and sizes and, although they are all marsupials, they can sometimes look quite different.

Marsupials are similar to other types of mammals, but one big difference is that most marsupials do not have a placenta. The placenta is inside female mammals and gives the unborn baby everything that it needs to grow and survive. Instead, marsupial young are born very early and feed on their mother's milk from inside the pouch.

Quokka

8

TAILS

Many marsupials have long, strong tails. Some marsupials, like kangaroos and wallabies, use their tails for balance as they jump. They can also use them to push themselves forward, like a fifth leg. The tail is so strong that it can hold the kangaroo's body weight without any support from the back legs.

Male kangaroos lean back on their tails to kick and fight other males.

Other marsupials, like opossums, have tails that can hold onto things like tree branches. This helps them move about in the trees. Their tails can even hold and carry objects.

Baby opossums can hang from branches using just their tails.

9

POUCHES

Nearly all female marsupials have a pouch. The pouch is a fold of skin that covers part of the mother's body.

The newborn baby joey crawls inside when it is very tiny and stays there for around eight months, where it is safe and warm. During this time, the joey feeds on its mother's milk, which makes it grow big and strong very quickly.

Young quokkas stay safe and warm in their mother's pouch.

Kangaroo pouches are **sticky** to help the joey stay inside and not fall out!

Most pouches, like the ones on kangaroos, are on the front of the animal and are open at the top. Wombat pouches, however, are closed at the top and open at the bottom. This is because wombats do lots of digging underground – if the pouch was open at the top it would fill up with dirt and soil, which would not be very nice for the joey!

PATAGIA

Some marsupials live high up in the forest <u>canopies</u>. They must travel from tree to tree to find food and escape from predators. Some trees are very far apart from each other, so these marsupials <u>evolved</u> to grow special bits of skin called patagia. The patagia act like wings and allow the animals to glide between the trees. There are seven species of gliding possum that use patagia to do this.

Sugar Glider

Patagia

Sugar gliders can cover distances of up to 148 feet (45 m) by gliding!

GETTING AROUND

Marsupials move around in different ways depending on their habitat. Marsupials that only live in trees, like sugar gliders and koalas, are called arboreal marsupials. Ones that live on the land, like kangaroos and wombats, are known as terrestrial marsupials.

Sugar Glider

Most terrestrial marsupials use their four legs to move across the ground. Kangaroos are different because they have two legs and two arms. They jump forward by using both feet at the same time. They can cover over 23 feet (7 m) in one jump, and can hop nearly 6.5 feet (2 m) up into the air.

Red Kangaroo

BREATHING

Marsupials are mammals. This means that they breathe using a pair of <u>organs</u> called lungs. Marsupials breathe in air through their nose and mouth. The air then fills up the lungs and flows into the <u>bloodstream</u>. Marsupials and other animals need <u>oxygen</u> from the air to survive.

Julia Creek Dunnart

When joeys are first born, their lungs are not fully developed and are still very weak. The newborn joeys of Julia Creek dunnarts have <u>permeable</u> skin. This means that they can breathe through their skin for the first few days until their lungs grow stronger.

PREDATORS AND PREY

All animals can be sorted into groups depending on what they eat. The three groups are carnivores, herbivores, and omnivores.

Marsupials can be herbivores, omnivores, or carnivores. They have different teeth depending on what food they eat. Tasmanian devils are carnivores and eat mostly snakes, birds, insects, and fish. They also eat dead animal carcasses, called carrion. Tasmanian devils have long canine teeth to tear off the meat easily.

Herbivores
Plant Eaters

Carnivores
Meat Eaters

Omnivores
Plant and Meat Eaters

Tasmanian Devil

Canine Teeth

Animals that hunt other animals are called predators, whereas animals that are hunted are called prey.

Tiger Quoll

The tiger quoll is a predator that hunts small animals like birds, rats, possums, and rabbits. Tiger quolls are also scavengers. This means that they eat the carrion of animals that other predators have killed first. Quolls are also the prey of larger predators like foxes, cats, and Tasmanian devils.

Some animals, like tiger quolls, are both **predator** and prey.

LAND, TREES, AND
BURROWS

Habitats are the homes of living things. They provide food and shelter for the plants and animals that live in them. Most marsupials live in Australia, but some live in North, South, and Central America.

Kangaroos and wallabies live on grasslands while marsupial moles burrow underground. Marsupial mice live on the forest floor and gliding possums like the sugar glider live in nests high up in the trees.

A **group** of **kangaroos** is called a **mob**.

A koala's favorite food is eucalyptus leaves. They spend all their time eating and sleeping, so they spend most of their lives sitting in eucalyptus trees where they can easily reach their food and stay safely hidden from predators on the ground.

Koalas are strong and have sharp claws. This helps them to grip onto tree branches so that they do not fall off.

Koalas can eat up to two pounds of eucalyptus leaves and sleep for 18 hours every day.

Eucalyptus Leaves

ADAPTATION 🐾

Many marsupials have adapted to their environments in amazing ways. Adaptations are changes that help an animal to survive.

Water opossums live in streams and lakes, and have evolved some useful features for living in water. Their fur is short and <u>water-repellent</u>, and their back feet are <u>webbed</u>, which makes them very good swimmers.

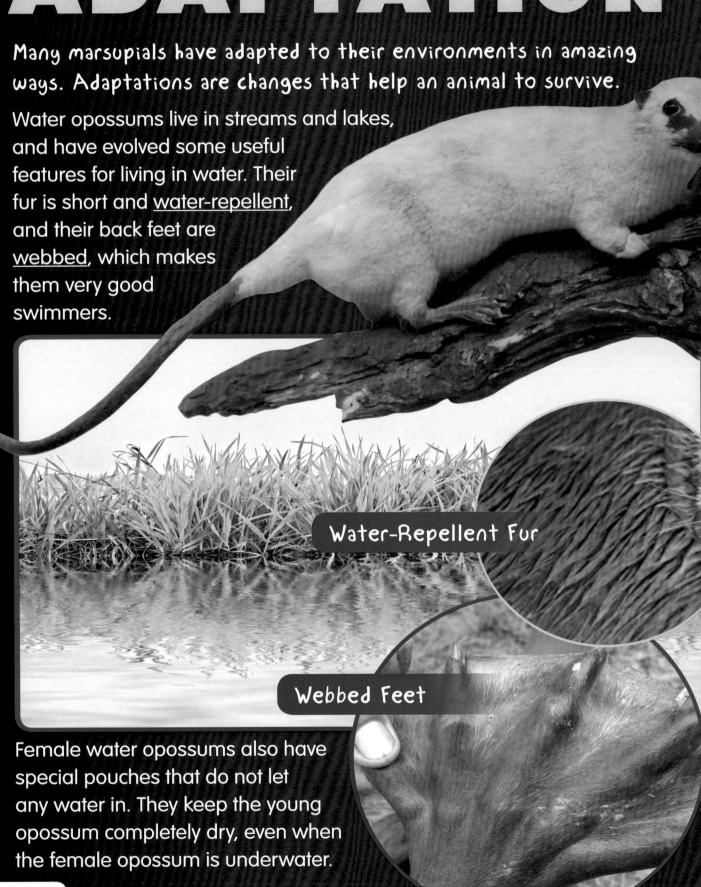

Water-Repellent Fur

Webbed Feet

Female water opossums also have special pouches that do not let any water in. They keep the young opossum completely dry, even when the female opossum is underwater.

Wombats are very good diggers and do lots of burrowing underground. When they are digging their burrows, they shovel dirt and soil towards their bodies. Wombats have a special adaptation that stops any soil from getting inside their pouch: they have backwards pouches that open towards the bottom. This means that the wombats can dig out their burrows and tunnels and the joeys can stay safe and clean. It is important that no dirt gets inside the pouch because the joey could <u>suffocate</u> and die.

This wombat is crawling out of its burrow.

Pouch Opening

LIFE CYCLES

The life cycle of an animal is the series of changes that it goes through from the start to the end of its life.

The life cycle of marsupials is very similar to the life cycle of other mammals. Both life cycles have a stage called reproduction, where <u>fertilization</u> takes place and the female becomes pregnant with a baby. Just like in other mammals, fertilization occurs inside the female marsupial's body and she then gives birth to live young. However, the newborn joeys are still very small, so they must stay in the female's pouch for several months after being born.

A young koala stays in its mother's pouch for around six months.

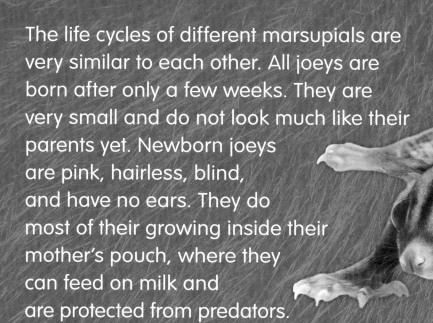

The life cycles of different marsupials are very similar to each other. All joeys are born after only a few weeks. They are very small and do not look much like their parents yet. Newborn joeys are pink, hairless, blind, and have no ears. They do most of their growing inside their mother's pouch, where they can feed on milk and are protected from predators.

Although they are **fish** and not **marsupials**, male **seahorses** also have a **pouch**. They hold their **eggs** inside the pouch for around **three weeks** until they **hatch**.

21

LIFE CYCLE OF A KANGAROO

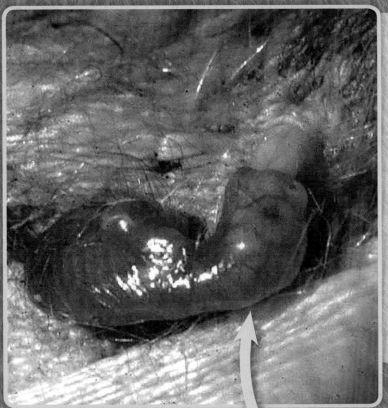

Kangaroos are the largest marsupials in the world. They live in the woodlands and grasslands of Australia and have one joey at a time. When the joey is born after around one month, it is only 0.8 inch (2 cm) long. It uses its front <u>limbs</u> to crawl through its mother's fur to reach the pouch. Newborn joeys are deaf and blind, so they use their sense of smell and touch to find the pouch.

Kangaroos become adults when they are around two years old. They are now big enough and old enough to have joeys of their own. Female joeys stay with their mothers, but male joeys leave to find a mob of their own.

The joey stays in its mother's pouch for up to eight months. It feeds on its mother's milk to grow big and strong. It starts to grow fur and ears and, after a few months, its eyes open. The joey can now start spending time outside of the pouch.

When it is around eight months old, the joey is too big for the pouch. It has grown a lot and can now explore further, but will still return to drink its mother's milk. The female kangaroo might now give birth to another joey, which crawls into her pouch. She can produce different milk for the two different joeys.

EXTREME
MARSUPIALS

VIRGINIA OPOSSUM

Venomous snakes are a big danger to mammals all over the world. They kill their prey by biting and injecting them with a harmful substance called venom. Virginia opossums are immune to snake venom. This means that they will not be harmed if they are bitten by a snake. Some scientists believe that we could use Virginia opossums to help produce an antivenom to protect humans from venomous snake bites.

Size:
Around 27.5 inches (70 cm) long

Home:
Woodlands in North America

Diet:
Fruit, insects, eggs, birds, reptiles, amphibians, and small mammals

KOALA

Koalas have a very strange diet. They are one of the few animals that can eat the leaves that grow on a eucalyptus tree. To most other animals, these leaves are very poisonous, but the koala's body can break down the leaves. This adaptation means that the koala doesn't have to fight many other animals for the eucalyptus leaves, because most other animals don't want to eat them.

Size:
23.5–33.5 inches (60-85 cm) long

Home:
Forests in eastern Australia

Diet:
Eucalyptus leaves

A koala has special teeth to eat the leaves.

WOMBAT

Wombats, like many other animals, are territorial. This means that they have their own area, or territory, that they guard against other animals. Territorial animals mark their territory with their scent to let other animals know that it is taken. Wombats do this by leaving <u>feces</u> around the area on top of rocks and logs, where other wombats can easily find it. They have cube-shaped feces, which can easily balance and not roll off.

Size:
Around 3.3 feet
(1 m) long

Home:
Underground burrows

Diet:
Grass

Wombat Feces

NUMBAT

Numbats are very small marsupials that feed mostly on one thing: termites. Termites are very small insects that are similar to ants. They live in nests and mounds on the ground and inside logs and trees. Numbats have a pointed head and a long <u>snout</u> they use to easily reach into small places. Their long, thin, sticky tongue is perfect for reaching into termite mounds. Adult numbats eat up to 20,000 termites every day.

Termite Mounds

Size:
7.8-10.6 inches (20–27 cm) long with a 4.7- to 10.6-inch (12–20 cm) tail!

Home:
Eucalyptus forests in Australia

Diet:
Termites

MARSUPIALS UNDER THREAT

Many species of marsupial are in danger of becoming <u>extinct</u>. One problem facing many of the animals in this book is deforestation.

Deforestation is when humans destroy forests either by cutting down the trees or by burning them. Forests are cleared to grow crops or to collect and use the wood. The Sulawesi bear cuscus is a marsupial that lives in the trees in Indonesia. So much of its habitat has been destroyed through deforestation that it is now a vulnerable species. This means that it could become extinct if deforestation continues.

Global warming is another problem that many marsupials face. Warmer temperatures can cause many habitats to disappear, making it difficult for the animals to survive. Mountain pygmy possums live high up in the mountains in Australia. As the temperature rises, the snow on top of the mountains will melt and could destroy their food and habitat.

Leadbeater's Possum

Warmer weather also leads to more wildfires. In 2009, around 45% of the Leadbeater's possum's habitat was destroyed in bushfires. There are now only between 50 and 2,000 of these animals left in the wild.

FIND OUT MORE

GO EXPLORING

Would you like to find out more about different species of marsupial? Or maybe even see some for yourself? Try visiting a zoo or a wildlife park to see what animals you can discover.

WEBSITES

GO WILD

www.gowild.wwf.org.uk

On this website you can follow links to information on all sorts of endangered animals and find out what WWF is doing to save wildlife.

BBC NATURE

www.bbc.co.uk/nature/life/ Diprotodontia

Learn about different species of marsupials and their habitats.

GLOSSARY

adapted	changed over time to suit the environment
antivenom	a type of medicine to protect against venom
bloodstream	the flow of blood in living things
canopies	the top layer of branches in a forest
carcasses	the bodies of dead animals
evolved	developed over a long time to become adapted to a certain habitat
extinct	when a species of animal is no longer alive
feces	the droppings, or poop, of an animal
fertilization	the process in which an egg can start to develop into a new living thing
global warming	the slow rise of the Earth's temperature
limbs	arms and legs, as well as the wings of birds
organs	parts of a living thing that have a specific, important functions
oxygen	a natural gas that all living things need in order to survive
permeable	something that allows liquid or gas to pass through it
premature	born early, or before the expected time
snout	the long nose and mouth of an animal
species	a group of very similar animals or plants that are capable of producing young together
suffocate	to die from a lack of air or being unable to breathe
unique	being the only one of its kind
vertebrate	an animal that has a backbone
warm-blooded	having a constant body temperature that stays warm
water-repellent	something that water cannot easily pass through
webbed	when toes or fingers are connected by skin
young	an animal's offspring

INDEX